D0548997

*My
Father's
Summers*

My
Father's
Summers

a daughter's memoir

Kathi Appelt

Henry Holt and Company
New York

Henry Holt and Company, LLC
Publishers since 1866
115 West 18th Street
New York, New York 10011
www.henryholt.com

Henry Holt is a registered trademark of Henry Holt and Company, LLC
Distributed in Canada by H. B. Fenn and Company, Ltd.

Library of Congress Cataloging-in-Publication Data
Appelt, Kathi
  My father's summers: a memoir / Kathi Appelt.
     p.   cm.
  Summary: A series of prose poems describes the author's life while she was growing up in
Houston, Texas, from her eleventh birthday in 1965 through her eighteenth in 1972, and
beyond.
  1. Appelt, Kathi, 1954– —Homes and haunts—Texas—Houston.
2. Authors, American—20th century—Family relationships. 3. Appelt, Kathi, 1954– —Child-
hood and youth. 4. Authors, American—20th century—Biography. 5. Houston (Tex.)—Social
life and customs. 6. Appelt, Kathi, 1954– —Family. [1. Appelt, Kathi, 1954– 2. Authors,
American. 3. Women—Biography. 4. Houston (Tex.)—Social life and customs.] I. Title.
PS3551.P5578Z468 2004   813'.54—dc22   [B]   2003056644

ISBN 0-8050-7362-0 / EAN 978-0-8050-7362-1
First Edition—2004 / Designed by Meredith Pratt
Printed in the United States of America on acid-free paper. ∞
10 9 8 7 6 5 4 3 2 1

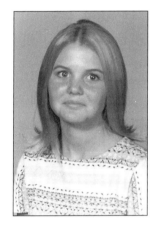 

To my beautiful sisters, Patti and B.J.

My
Father's
Summers

Birthday, 1965 – Eleven

On my eleventh birthday, he sent a letter written on
thin paper, airmail all the way from Arabia. When I held
it up to the light, I could see through it, see the lamp on
my bedroom ceiling. "Dear Bean," he wrote, my pet
name given to me when I was in the second grade. One
night he came home from work; he asked me, "How's it
going, Old Bean?" which made me burst into laughter,
his laughter too, caught by surprise, and ever after I was
his one and only Bean. I forgot what the rest of the
letter said, the only important word being the one he
saved for me, his oldest daughter. Maybe he signed it
"With love." Maybe he sent a rupee, tucked neatly
inside the folds. Maybe he didn't say anything else.
"Dear Bean" was enough.

Calling

Eleven months is a long time for one father to be gone. Floating around in the desert, sending letters that took two weeks to arrive, once in a while calling, his voice ringing through the cable that lay at the bottom of the Atlantic Ocean. Miles and miles of cable. Between sentences you could hear the waves wash over the wires, washing his voice until it didn't even sound like him. He could only talk for a few minutes, almost all of them to my mother. When I did get a turn, I didn't know what to say, only wanted to feel his words bumping against my ear, wondered if the fish swimming by could hear us, could know about this girl in Texas, missing her father half a world away.

First Ever

It was my first birthday without him. The middle of the summer. He wasn't supposed to be gone so long. "Only a few months," he said. Then he left, a winter morning so early the sun didn't see him go, only my mother and her three daughters waving from the window of the airport as he boarded the plane. Up it flew, all the way to the oil fields of the Persian Gulf, to a barge atop the deep blue sea, atop a billion barrels of crude, floating there, away from us. My mother didn't change her sheets for two weeks, not wanting to lose his scent. One morning I awoke before her and found her still asleep, arms wrapped around his pillow, her breath soft, cat at her feet.

The Guitar

Because he loved the Kingston Trio and the Four
Seasons and all those groups who sang songs like "The
Streets of Laredo," where the cowboy dies, shot through
the heart, not only by a bullet but by love, unrequited;
and because the songs were accompanied by a guitar, my
mother decided that I, her oldest, should learn to play
guitar, so she bought me one from Sears for twenty-five
dollars. On Saturday afternoons, she took me to the
music store where a tall boy with a quiet smile tried to
teach me how to play "Wildwood Flower." My fingers
were clumsy on the strings, and they ached after only a
few minutes. I think the tall boy knew that guitar would
not be my avenue to fame and fortune, but my mother
reminded me about how much my father loved the music.
So each night in my room, I strummed the three
chords—C, G, and F—over and over, sending them into
the air of my bedroom, sending them out through the
window, into the evening. There is a snake charmer in

Bombay who plays his flute beside the snake's basket. There the snake, sleeping soundly, becomes hypnotized by the notes and gradually uncoils himself, slides up into the daylight, wanting the music, wanting it. I was the snake charmer's sister, pulling my father toward me with the only three chords I knew. A guitar is not a flute, but the yearning was the same.

Saved

We saved things for him. My sister Patti saved whatever she could hold in her palm—rocks, pennies, bottle caps. With the pennies she planned to save enough to buy a plane ticket to go see him. How many pennies would it take? Photographs, report cards, jokes, songs, stories, we even saved Christmas. Long after my mother took down the tree, his gifts sat in the corner of the living room. Every so often, we shook them. The shoe box with new Hush Puppies, the skinny box with the tie, the small box of cuff links—the one that made the most noise. Even the fudge my grandmother made. After a while the bright red and green paper faded from the daylight that streamed in through the window, but it was such a slow fading no one noticed until the night he finally opened them and the paper that had been folded under and taped down was several shades redder and greener. But we didn't know this while he was gone, while we rattled the hopeful boxes. And he was gone a long time.

Thoroughbreds

They're a breed of horse that began in Arabia with a
single stallion, the Godolphin. They say when he ran, no
one could see him. They say he was temperamental, that
his hooves were sharp as knives, that he might bite off
your ear if you got too close. But there was a stable boy
who slept in his stall and loved him so much he could
handle him with a halter made only of ribbons. There are
things we ache for, aren't there? A horse, a father, the
wind. While he was in Arabia, I dreamed that my father
lived with horses, raced them back and forth beneath a
million Arabian stars, whispered in their silky ears about
his daughter who loved them so.

Sizes

When someone turns up missing, there is always
a description of the clothing. "Boy last seen wearing
a green T-shirt and white shorts." "The woman wore a
white cotton dress with blue flowers." "Dorothy had on
a pinafore and black Mary Janes." (This would have
been before the good fairy gave her those ruby slippers.)
My favorite pajamas with the feet in them fit when my
father left. They fit for many months after he left. But
one month became another became another. Soon he was
gone for over a year and into the next. Nothing I could
wear when he left fit anymore, especially the pajamas.
All my pants legs were too short. Zippers wouldn't zip.
Skirts were too tight. What if it was me who turned up
missing? Could he find me with these different clothes,
these bigger feet, all this new skin and bone and hair?

Once, Before

When I was seven my mother gave me a Sleeping Beauty doll. She had golden blond hair and a blue satin dress, and when I laid her on my bed, her blue eyes closed. She seemed to glow, all blond and blue and sleeping, waiting for her prince. She wouldn't change in a million years, no matter how long it took for the prince to get there. But my mother changed. She learned how to pay the bills, how to drive us to the beach alone, how to set up the tent and take it down, how to cook swordfish. She was good at waiting. She glowed too.

The Club

We were my father's club, my mother, Patti and B.J.
and I. We were my father's own faithful foursome. We
played his records on the stereo. We sang his favorite
songs. We ate his favorite fried shrimp and baked
potatoes. We read his favorite poems by Rudyard Kipling
out loud to each other. When we saw a cowboy movie we
said, "Daddy would like that." When we heard a new
tune on the radio we said, "Daddy prefers the Four
Seasons." When we went to a restaurant we said, "They
don't chop the lettuce the way Daddy likes it." We
thought we knew what he liked and what he didn't.

Before, at the Monument

In the middle of the prairie south of Houston, the
San Jacinto Monument rises into the sky, 570 feet, an
obelisk. One Sunday my father took us there to see
where Sam Houston's army routed Santa Anna and his
soldiers. I was seven, no more than eight. There's a star
on the top of the monument, and you can ride the
elevator all the way up and stand just below its five
points; for a nickel you can look through the telescopes,
mounted in concrete with brass bolts. And what you'll
see is a hundred miles of oil refineries, huge tanks,
coiling pipes, smokestacks. You'll see the Ship Channel,
its giant ships moored at the docks. You'll see the
buildings of downtown rising into the clouds. That's if
you look out. It's what they fought for. But if you look
directly down, there will be the tops of oak trees,
growing in a park where all those soldiers died, where

the old generals shook hands and Texas stopped being Mexico. What I remember most was the way the building rocked when the wind blew, how my father held on to my hand. "It's a long way down, isn't it, Bean?" he said. And then, I'll never forget: "If we held hands, we'd surely fly."

Expectations

It would go like this: a date would be set, say in two or
three weeks. As the date got nearer, my mother stripped
and waxed the kitchen floor. It took her all morning, first
the warm soapy water, then the stripper, then more warm
water, the wax. And drying in between. She gave my
sisters and me a handful of old rags, and we poured
Old English furniture polish on each piece of wooden
furniture—the coffee table, the side tables, our chests of
drawers—we rubbed the thick brown polish into the wood
until it shone. We cleaned the windows with vinegar and
water and old newspapers. My mother swept out the
garage and then sprayed the concrete floor with the
garden hose. The house gleamed. My mother sighed and
poured Jergens hand lotion onto her hands, rough from
soap and wax. Then off to the A&P for fresh green
beans and a pound of shrimp and a can of cherries to

make a pie, and phone calls to all our relatives. We polished all of our shoes, even my father's, the ones he left behind. Patti drew new pictures. B.J. brushed the dog. I practiced my guitar, made sure it was in tune. That's how it would go.

Then

It would go like this: A knock on the door. A man from Western Union.

"PlansdelayedSTOPMoreworkSTOPGotraiseSTOP BehomefourmonthsSTOPLoveyougirlsSTOP."

That's how it would go. Stop.

Parakeet

Before he came home, my grandmother bought me a green parakeet. I named him Johnny Dan. Every afternoon after school I took his cage from its hook and sat it on my bed. Then I talked to him in my softest voice. Finally, I put my hand in through the cage door. The first time he startled and flew helplessly against the side of the cage, furiously flapping his wings. I quickly withdrew my hand, afraid he'd tear his fragile wings. We did this for days—hand in cage, furious flapping, hand out of cage. And then one day, I tried again and he climbed onto my outstretched finger, perched there as if it was the most normal thing in the world. His tiny claws bit into the skin of my finger, but they didn't hurt, and it didn't matter if they did. When a green parakeet perches on your finger, it doesn't matter whether your father is coming home or not.

Sunrise

First, there was the phone call so deep in the night it
seemed to crack the air, my mother's voice, crying. I was
already sitting up in bed when she switched on the light.
"He's coming home," she said, tears running down her
face. "He'll be here in three days." Second, there was
the wild dance we did together, waking my sisters,
waking the dog, waking the parakeet in his cage, who
whistled, whistled, whistled. Third, there was the sun
that came up, having already shone on my father in the
middle of the Persian Gulf. Home. Come home.

Proof

We polished my mother's convertible, a gift, the "best gift ever," she said, proof of his affection, needing that proof. That night we'd drive to the airport with the top down, we'd let the warm Houston air blow through our hair, we'd find him on the tarmac and bring him back down the city streets that led to our house. Two summers before, when he rolled it into our driveway, from the kitchen window my mother watched, dropped the glass she was washing, chipping the edge on the porcelain sink, and ran outside. Never mind that her hands were still wet, soap suds wrapped around her wedding ring, she touched the car door like she did when she tested the iron, waited for it to hiss. Whenever I watched her tap her wet finger against its blazing surface, her courage gripped me, made a small flame. My father opened the door, stepped out into her arms. "Oh honey, oh honey," she said over and over. We sisters couldn't quit jumping. My father held the door for her as she slid behind the steering wheel, put it in reverse, and backed out, all of us watching her go. Back in the kitchen, he pulled a cold Black Label from the refrigerator. He never noticed the unwashed dishes, the glass with the chip, never saw the bubbles melt, forgot there were three small jumping daughters by the driveway, waiting.

The Song

Nights and nights of practice on my guitar all added up to one moment, my father sitting across from me, the smoke from his cigarette a halo above his head. He was still on Arabia Time, not quite awake, not quite asleep, almost there. My left hand shook as my fingers tried hard to find the right frets, press the right strings against the neck. All those evenings in my room added up to a single song: "My Old Kentucky Home." I don't know why that was the one I picked out of all the songs I had practiced. Maybe it was because I found the music printed on the side of a box of Kentucky Fried Chicken? Maybe it was just because of home, Kentucky, Houston, here? That would be the obvious answer. I think it had more to do with horses. To a girl who loves them Kentucky is heaven. Blue grass, white fences, running so fast that as you go by, you are only a blur, a streak of speed, a tiny moment. A tiny moment when your father says, "How beautiful."

Stepping Out

Here's the thing. He didn't really come home at all. He only lingered there long enough to unpack and then pack again. A few days. When his best friend, Choice Roy, drove up to get him, he looked over his shoulder and cried. I tried to cry too, surprised that I couldn't. But here's the other thing: I was already used to missing him.

Aromas

What I wasn't used to was having his smell back, the smoke from his Camel cigarettes, his Old Spice After Shave, the shoe polish he used on his boots. All those father odors, filling up the house. My mother opened every window, waxed the wooden furniture, sprayed room freshener in every corner. She scrubbed the tiles on the bathroom floor, scrubbed the dog's water bowl, scrubbed her hair, her hands, her face, shiny. Then she sat in her convertible and wept it all away, all but the smell. "I can't scrub the air," she said. And so he was there, but not really. Where was he?

Before, When We Were Cowboys

Sunday evenings it was the Cartwright brothers,
Adam, Hoss, and Little Joe, in black-and-white atop
their mounts, and the Lone Ranger and Tonto, running,
running, running across the screen with the "William
Tell Overture" in the background; they settled the
western end of our living room. Not alone. They were
joined by Wyatt and Rowdy and the Virginian. Have
gun, will travel. So we did. Each day my sisters and I
saddled up our invisible steeds and galloped over the
prairies, through the rocky canyons, across the Red
River, the territory of our front yard and most of the
front yards on Mayo Avenue. On hot afternoons we
killed all the bandits and went to live with the Nez Percé.
It was the horses, prancing, tails high, who gave us
courage. But the guns helped too—dangerous, shiny.
After each shot we blew across both barrels to cool them

down, especially when there was a neighborhood shoot-out with the twins across the street, a particularly gruesome twosome named Kevin and Keith, lawbreakers, fit for a hanging, hard to believe they were twins, one so fair, the other so dark.

The Fair Twin

Sometime after my father left again, Kevin the fair twin set all the invisible horses loose, opened the gates, untethered their legs, said they needed to roam free. I distrusted Kevin then, thought he might also open the way for the parakeet, the one who lived in a cage in my room and sang to the sun each morning. As it turns out, Kevin loved the parakeet more than the horses. There's something to be said for visibility, something about being easier to love.

The Dark Twin

He asked me to the Sunday-school party. Keith. Even though it wasn't a real date, neither of us old enough. But we had been friends for all our memories. It would be practice. It would be a pretend date. There would be punch and cookies and a flower corsage. My grandmother bought the material for a brand-new dress. But his mother stepped in. There's a difference between a girl whose father is gone because he's working and a girl whose father is gone for "other reasons."

Signs

His best friend was Choice Roy. Friends before my mother, before me, before my two younger sisters. Choice. A painter, an artist, he earned a living by painting signs, the kind we saw along the Gulf Freeway that led from downtown Houston to the middle of Galveston and back, the kind we noticed on the way to the beach. There he drew designs in the wet sand and then watched as the foamy waves erased them. He didn't care. They were crabs and fish and seashells. And shouldn't they be in the sea anyway? he said. He was our Choice, the way he drew small animals on the paper napkins in restaurants, the way he laughed at my father's jokes, his billboards along the freeway—Eat at Guido's, Mack's Auto Parts, The Tastee-Freez—the perfect letters bold against the Houston sky, jumping into our headlights as we turned the corner. He's the one who painted my mother's name on the side of her convertible. Choice. Before. After. As if there was one. Driving my father away.

Before

When I was nine, my parents borrowed my grandmother's new Ford Mustang because it had air-conditioning and because my grandmother insisted, and because there was no way our old Chevy could make the two thousand miles from our house on Mayo Avenue in Houston to Decker, Montana, where my father's old Army buddy owned a sheep ranch. Even his name was Buddy. Old Army buddy Buddy. It was the first day after third grade at Pearl Rucker Elementary School, and I held the bag of peppermints Mrs. Dodge had given me, along with a note: "Thank you for being my star this year." I didn't like peppermints, but they were from Mrs. Dodge, and I loved Mrs. Dodge. So my two younger sisters wouldn't get a single one for the whole drive there and back. We drew imaginary boundaries on the vinyl seat and dared each other to cross them. Somewhere outside Amarillo, me riding behind him, my father rolled down his window to throw out his cigarette butt, flicked it with his thumb and middle finger, not hard enough because it bounced against the car and flew back inside, landed on my new red shorts—the ones my mother made just the week before on my grandmother's old Singer sewing machine, her foot pumping the iron treadle as she smiled at the neat straight stitches—the fabric barely saved the soft skin of my thigh, the cigarette made a hole the size of a dime. My father slammed the brakes, swerved when I screamed, then pulled over to the side of the road, jerked open the door, and pulled me out. "Don't you ever cut loose like that when I'm driving!" he yelled, not noticing the tiny brown burn on my shorts. Once back on the road, he lit up another cigarette, looked at my mother, small beside him in the seat, his voice demanding, "Can't you teach these girls to behave?" He turned up the air conditioner. I breathed in the smoke, looked out the window and saw only sky, dreamed the Mustang was real, that I could gallop away, warm air in my hair, silky mane in my face, no imaginary boundaries. Be a star. Learn to love peppermints. Each mile after that a wish for cutting loose.

Sand

He called again from Arabia, said he'd stay there for a while. "We'll sort this all out," he told me. "You'll see, Bean." There it was again, my private name. I thought I could hear the sand blowing against his khaki pants.

Whispers

There were whispers coming from my mother, pieces of information not fully formed, not thoroughly bound by the edges of whole words, partial bits of language caught sometimes between the sofa cushions, under the coffee table, above the cabinets, lying here and there. I'd hear them whenever the screen door slammed each time we walked through, floating just beneath my touch, audible but not. It's the way of whispers to slip under the mat at the kitchen sink and hide behind the spices in the cupboard. There but not there. Heard but not quite. There were whispers afoot, coming from my mother.

Other Reasons

The insinuation was that she must have treated him badly. There were rumors that she didn't satisfy him. The word on the street was that she just wasn't a good wife. What was it that my mother did wrong?

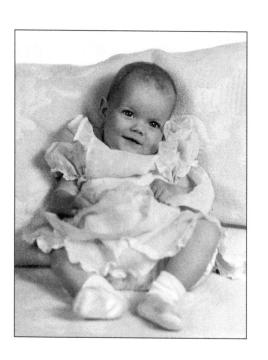

Long Before

After I was born, he was stationed in El Paso at Fort Bliss. "All you had to do was sigh," my mother said, "and the sand would kick up into a dust devil." It must have been all sand except for a few cottonwood trees. Our house on the Army base was a carbon copy of a hundred other houses. "When I hung your diapers out to dry," she told me, "the sand coated them." She paused. "They seemed to glisten, the diapers."

Leavings

There are different kinds of leavings. There was the first kind, the one where certainty stayed behind and sat at our table, watched TV with us, fed the dog, made a big promise. It was a General MacArthur kind of leaving. "I shall return." Like that. And we believed. But the old general didn't, did he? So here we were, adrift. That was the second kind of leaving, the one where he took certainty along for the ride. Once we could say, "When Daddy comes home . . . ," and now those words left our language, made a hole in the lexicon. And there was a new word we had to get ahold of: *bewildered.*

Rearrangements

Bewilderment creates its own energy, and my mother
tapped into hers by rearranging the house, moving the
furniture, the pictures on the walls, my father's record
albums that lined the hallway by the front door. Each
chair, each bed, each table found a new home. The
Kingston Trio moved into the closet. My sisters and I
suffered, bumping into the coffee table in its new spot,
rounding a corner and coming face-to-face with a shelf
that wasn't there before. Our house was a new country,
familiar but not. The dog, especially, couldn't seem to
get comfortable. "Because he's the only male in the
house," said my mother, her voice edgy. The dog, a
German shepherd mix named Sam, whined and tucked
his tail between his legs. She painted the walls in the den
soft pink, a color she was sure my father wouldn't like.
"It's not a man color," she said, "and we have no men
here." The pink walls made it so. So soft. One woman
and three girls, living in a house turning pink. My bed,

no longer in the corner, now stood in the very middle of the room, like a boat on a pond. At night, I could drop my line and fish for whatever lay beneath the rug, beneath the floor, beneath the dirt. If the line proved true, would it sink all the way to China?

Chinese Food

She quit cooking from scratch, and instead we ate
things from boxes and cans and even the freezer.
Banquet potpies. Del Monte spinach. Instant potatoes.
Our favorite, Chinese from a box, a kit with canned
chow mein and a cellophane bag of crispy noodles that
were so salty they made our mouths ache for more. She
put all her trust in packages, all our food in neat rows in
the cabinet, the refrigerator, the pantry; something
certain, freeze-dried and unspoiled, able to outlast the
winter, survive any blow.

Birthday, 1966 – Twelve

He sent me a bottle of Coca-Cola with the white name written in Arabic. I traced the letters with my finger, smooth against the green glass. They reminded me of the script you might find on the side of Aladdin's magic lamp, and maybe there was a genie, invisible, able to breathe under soda. Who could say if it really spelled "Coca-Cola"? He told me it was a little different from the American version. How could it be any other way? How could a Coca-Cola taste the same in such a different tongue? If my father wrote my name in Arabic, would I know who I was? Wouldn't I be a different daughter? If he said, "I love you, Bean," in a language besides the one between us, would I understand? I didn't dare open the bottle, didn't set the genie free, couldn't bear the loss.

Same Birthday, 1966

For my twelfth birthday, my mother gave me a razor, thick heavy metal, the kind with the handle that twists to open twin doors on the top, and then twists to close again, trapping the menacing double-edged blade. In the bathtub, I propped my foot up on the edge and coated my leg, the right one, with a thick layer of Noxema shaving cream, the same kind she used. Starting at the ankle, I pulled the blade toward my knee, making a clear road along my skin, then dipping the razor into the water. I watched as the clouds of foam melted on the water's surface, leaving a thin layer of soap and hair. At last I would shed my furry legs, I would be just like the girls in *Teen* magazine. I would dazzle all the boys at the swimming pool with my sleek shins and soft calves, then I would throw back my head and laugh at them whenever they approached. Such boys. Another road, another dip, and then like a stripe down the middle of a highway, a red line where the skin had come off, all the way from

ankle to knee, so quick I never saw it, never felt it, until
the foam began to turn pink, and then in a flash, my leg
was on fire. Blood dripped into the water. I climbed
out of the tub and wrapped it with the pink towel that
matched the pink walls and the pink shower curtain and
the pink bath mat, all so pink. Then sat on the toilet seat
and sobbed, one leg half shaved, the other still furry, all
those boys at the pool sneering at me, half girl, half
there.

Even Before My Father

All families have histories. My father's grandfather was a wheelwright. He repaired the wooden wheels on carriages and carts. His shop was in an old Houston neighborhood called the Heights. There's a newspaper story about him in the *Houston Press,* a paper that no longer exists, about the storm of 1900, the one where the water washed over Galveston Island and carried away six thousand people. My great-grandfather found everyone he knew who owned a cart, all his customers. They hitched them to draft horses and mules and drove to Galveston. There they helped gather the bodies of the dead, placed them in huge piles, and set them on fire. "To keep disease from spreading," my father told me, and he was told by his mother who wasn't even born then. My father never met his grandfather, but he loved him nonetheless. We can love people even when we can't see them. We can.

More Whispers

Whispers, whispers slipping around the furniture, caught in drawers, padding down the hallway late at night, louder each day. A word that was making itself better known: *divorce*. And now the whispers were coming from aunts, uncles, my grandparents. It's an ugly word, isn't it? Its only true rhyme: *remorse*.

Definition

What it meant: neighbors holding my sisters and me, my mother, at arm's length, no longer a family in a family neighborhood; teachers looking at us with sidelong glances; no-longer-welcome signs coming from other parents; fewer invitations to birthday parties and sleepovers; lots of sentences with *sorry* at the end. Single-mother household. Same thing as a disease. The divorce disease. Seems we scared people. What if they caught it too?

What It Also Meant

My mother had to get a job.

Adjustments

When my mother went to work, we three came home to a place without her. This was a new kind of leaving— leaving us alone in the hours after school. In charge of preparing dinner, cleaning our rooms, vacuuming the den, feeding the dog, doing our own laundry. She had no patience for chores left undone, couldn't stand to come home to a mess, left no room for sloppiness. We each had a key. We could no longer go outdoors after school, had to stay inside until she got home, sometimes after dark, and then it was too late to go out; had to call her the minute we got there, had to get all our homework done, had to learn to lock ourselves in.

Before, Again

Second grade brought with it a new lunch box with My Friend Flicka on its metal face, new crayons and manila paper, a new package of pencils, a hurricane named Carla. The sky turned green, the wind sprinted across our yard, and early in the evening began to bay, a thousand hounds cut loose. My father moved our beds away from the windows. When morning came, and we looked outside, it was water, water everywhere, waves lapping against the top steps. The houses looked like boats, barely moored to their cement foundations. Rooftop shingles tore off in groups of two and three and flew like birds, throwing themselves into trees, bent over and broken, cracked in half. The rain blew sideways, driving itself like nails into the wooden slats of the house. The dog whined, curled into a tight ball under the kitchen table, refused to come out. When it was all over, a hundred crawdad mounds, like pyramids, covered the muddy grass, black as ebony. We dug up a dozen, the same size as our thumbs, and put them in my sister's wagon, filled it with water, and made small crawdad islands. Strips of bacon and dog food are what we fed them. For days we took them on trips around the neighborhood. The next week mosquitos rose from the ground in black clouds, the city sent out fogging trucks. Up and down our streets they sprayed their sweet-smelling poison while my sisters and I and the other kids in the neighborhood ran after them, enchanted, fading in and out of one another's sight, our skin coated with a thin layer of silvery moisture, thinner than sweat, thinner than mist, thinner than the smoke from my father's cigarette.

Wedding Pictures

My mother looked like a fairy, barely five feet tall. Her white dress came to her ankles and she wore white ballet slippers. He wore white too with a black bow tie. Black and white. There was no in-between. They both said I do. They agreed. They promised. It was all there, in black and white.

How They Met

At Foley's in downtown Houston. She was on her way down the escalator—shy, petite, her white blouse starched, her shoes patent leather, hair curled back in a bob—and he was on the way up. When he saw her, he jumped over the moving rail and stood right next to her, going down, down, down, falling, falling, falling in love.

Wishing Star

I stood in the driveway, dusk falling all around me, and there it was, the first evening star, the one you wish upon, the one that urges you to say what it is you want. I have seen the reflection of stars in water, quivering, as if the wishes they held made them vibrate. Once all my wishes were horses, Appaloosas, paints, chestnuts, their sharp hooves digging into the soft earth beneath us. Once I was the queen of the rodeo, star girl. But now, I stand there; new stars popping holes into the night sky until soon it looks like a paper doily, the kind we always have on Valentine's Day, when the teacher places a sugar cookie in front of you and a paper cup of red Hawaiian Punch, and all I want, all I ever wanted, was for him to come back, to take my mother's hand again, to stop all the whispers. So there it was: the newest wish.

Before, at Easter

Always, each year, the week before Easter, my grandmother took us to that same Foley's downtown to buy our Easter dresses, frilly frocks with lace and huge bows in the back. We looked like pastel bells, our thin legs bumping against the full skirts, chiming. Then lunch at Sakowitz, egg-salad sandwiches and cheese biscuits so light it seemed if you let go of them between the dish and your mouth, they might float up and bump against the ceiling. Next it was Woolworth's, the best, where there were a thousand multicolored chicks in the window display. Puffs of red, orange, blue, pink, green, their peeps surrounded us, called us. My grandmother bought one for each of us. We brought them home in a cardboard box and set them in the garage next to the dryer where they would stay warm. We loved them for a week, but as they grew, they lost their puffy feathers and turned regular chicken colors—brown and white. Only my sister Patti continued to adore them. Long past

Easter, she became their mother hen, taught them to rest on her shoulder, took them for rides in her wagon. They followed her everywhere. She tried to hide them in her room, but it's hard to keep chickens quiet. "They need a farm," my father told her. He had a friend who had a place. She missed the chickens, she did. She didn't know it was a practice missing.

Then There Was the Cat

She wandered up one day and helped herself to Sam's food, just like that. Sam, who had always barked at cats, let this one eat from his bowl. She was small and calico and in a matter of days delivered four kittens in our garage, right beside the dryer where the chickens had once lived. We called her Cozy because she made herself so comfortable in our family. We named the kittens for the seasons—Spring, Autumn, Winter, and Summer. Then one day Cozy disappeared, leaving us with the kittens. More practice missing.

I Made Three

There is a photograph of my mother and father. He's in the Army, the Eighty-second Airborne, his hat is cocked to the side. My mother sits on his lap. Her face is round, and her smile is wide. She's radiant. "You're in there too, Bean," he told me. And I was. Still bearing gills, I was a tiny mergirl, swimming away inside my mother: small, safe, warm, invisible. It's clear the three of us are happy.

Three Too

There is another photo of my sisters and me. It's summer and we are playing in the swimming pool, the kind whose sides our father had to blow into forever before it would stand up and hold water. The three of us are wearing only underwear, but we are so small it doesn't matter. Patti and I are standing up, but B.J. is squinting squarely into the camera, which my father is holding. Only my body is there, my father having left my head out of the frame. We are so much the same, so much alike. When one of us cries, the other two join in, a spontaneous crying. It's the same with laughing. It's the same. We are.

Birthday, 1967 – Thirteen

Thirteen. From overseas he sent a plastic Polaroid camera for my birthday, a Swinger. I used up all my birthday money buying film. The photos were grainy and out of focus, except for the one I took of my cousin when he jumped off the diving platform at the neighborhood pool. That one was clear, my cousin upside down, long legs akimbo, fingers just touching the water. When I squinted, it looked like he was balancing himself on the water, holding himself upright on the very tips of his fingers, that the water was solid, impenetrable. And that's what it felt like with my father, the water between us impenetrable. He was half a world away, grainy, out of focus, right at the tips of my fingers.

Before Another

When a father leaves for three years, a girl moves into her own fatherless style, a tight frenzy of scattered steps. But long before that, he took her to the beach, showed her the dunes where the crabs lived. At dusk, they began to emerge from their small caves and headed for the sea, their zigzag scampers so quick I could barely see them in the faltering light. He caught one in a coffee can, then held it out to me on the palm of his hand. As I reached for it, the crab retreated into its bumpy shell. It was so tiny, smaller than my fist. "When he gets bigger, he'll leave this shell behind and find another," he said. And that's what my father did. He found another.

Another

Her hair was dark. My mother's was fair. Her complexion was olive. My mother's was light. Her eyes were brown. My mother's were blue. She smoked incessantly. My mother didn't smoke at all. She didn't like to read. My mother read all the time. Her favorite color was green. My mother loved all colors. "Sometimes I love pink, sometimes I love blue," she said. Her name was Ann. My mother's middle name was Ann. My middle name was Ann; I added an *e*.

Short Skirts

At school, there was a rule about skirts. They had to touch the floor when you knelt on the ground. It must have been the same rule they had when my mother went to that school eighteen years before me. In 1967 skirts were short. Very short. None of mine hit the floor. My favorite was yellow vinyl, no washing required. I simply had to wipe it off with a damp cloth, the same way I wiped off the kitchen table after dinner. I wore it with bright yellow fishnet stockings and clunky black shoes. My leather purse with fringe on it hung lower than my skirt, swished against my legs when I walked, sang with every step. I learned to sashay. That's what my mother called it when I walked away from her, hips swinging from one side to the other, yellow skirt flashing down the halls.

The White Mouse

Patti collected pets—Easter chickens, kittens, goldfish, minnows, crawdads, lizards, puppies. One day she brought home a white mouse, a gift. Its coat was so white it was startling, and its eyes were the same bright pink as its tail and nose. In its tiny cage was an exercise wheel. The mouse ran for hours, never getting anywhere. We were hypnotized by it, running and running, hour after hour, the wheel throbbing. Once Patti took it out of the cage and handed it to me. I could feel its pounding heart beating against the tip of my finger. Running and running. By then it had run maybe a thousand miles. How many miles had my father run?

Mysteries

Wasn't he supposed to be on a barge in the middle of the blue Persian Gulf, drilling for oil, measuring the volume of the golden substance that rushed to the surface, pushed its way up out of the sandy bottom of the sea, took fathers from daughters? Wasn't he traipsing across the desert in white clothes to deflect the overbearing sun? Hadn't he dined on dates and olives, hearts of palm? Where did he find her? And her sons? Didn't he find them too?

Puzzle

Hide-and-seek, lost and found, ollie ollie oxen free, a game of tag-you're-it—and she was it. Turns out that my father's absence wasn't always a great distance, wasn't really as far away as the Middle East, but only an hour's drive from our house to hers. Still east. Turns out there were secret trips across the Atlantic Ocean. Secret trips across town. Here but not here. Close to home but not. With her and not us. Not us. Turns out he missed her more. If it were all a crossword puzzle, the clues would be: one down, two across. The blanks weren't hard to fill in.

Witnesses

There wasn't a wedding. My father said they simply went to the courthouse and got married by the justice of the peace. Said Choice went with them because they needed a witness. I was a witness too. Saw the cat give birth to four kittens. Saw my cousin do a flip off the high dive. Saw a storm roll in at the beach, watched the sky turn from blue to gray so that soon I couldn't tell where the rain ended and the sea began. Saw my mother double over in the middle of the driveway, saw her reach for the missing car, saw her tears slide down her face. I was a witness too.

Dominoes

When you line them all up in an S, one behind the other, it only takes the flick of a finger to make them fall. It was *s* for *sister.* I grabbed on to Patti grabbed on to B.J. On her finger, the gold band gleamed. We had always been sisters to sisters. And now we were sisters to brothers. Danny and Dwayne. They had always been brother to brother. Now brothers to sisters. Much younger than the three of us, small like their mother, now shared. They called her Mama. What were we supposed to call her?

Before, at the Rodeo

Each year in February the Houston Fat Stock Show and Rodeo was held at the old coliseum downtown. First there was a parade, cowboys, cowgirls, longhorn steers, clowns, huge balloons fastened to ropes and pulled by firemen, the cavalry, and always Foley's built a float—a flatbed trailer covered with crepe paper and pulled by a tractor, usually a John Deere. And then there was the fat stock show; 4-H-er's brought their calves and pullets, their fryers and boars, presented them to the judges for ribbons and cash. At last, the rodeo. When I was nine, the guest of honor was Michael Landon—"Little Joe"— hero of heroes, atop his beautiful paint horse, the same horse that galloped across our television screen every Sunday evening. The paint. My father promised to take us to the coliseum where they kept the paint in a stall. There we could stand, inches away, could breathe in his horse smell, look into his deep brown eyes. So close. Such a paint. But something happened. The day before we went, a fully grown man stuck his hand through the fence, wanted to pet the paint despite the signs that told him not to, just had to touch the brown-and-white coat, so silky, so soft. Seems the paint knew what the signs meant and so bit the man's hand, taking a finger right off and dropping it at the bottom of his stall. Nobody blamed the paint. But my father wouldn't take us there anymore. "I love all of your fingers, Bean," he said. I never blamed the paint.

Blame

You remove the small *e* and you have *blam.* The word shows up in comic books, where the superhero zooms in, sees the girl in her skintight red dress, huge boobs busting out in front, tied down on a railroad track or a conveyer belt that's headed toward a giant saw blade, the villain hovering over her with a haughty sneer, and *blam,* right in the poker. Saved again. It's different from *blame,* which was being tossed back and forth, my mother bitter, my father silent. But it carried a punch anyway.

Karen

Somewhere in the middle of all this, I found Karen. She didn't care that my mother was alone. Didn't mind that my father was gone. Couldn't care less about either of my parents. Together we spent the seventh grade at Deady Junior High School, a school as old as Houston itself, just a mile or so from the Ship Channel where a thousand ships a month moored, bearing steel from Germany, radios from Japan, and oil from Arabia. She played the piano. I played the flute. No more guitar. We played together in the orchestra; our director, Mrs. Moore, was the same director who had taught my father, the one who showed him how to play the trumpet. It was something I didn't know. That my father played the trumpet. It was something shared.

Dark Shadows

It was Karen who told me about *Dark Shadows*, with its heroine, Victoria Winters, trapped in a basement by the vampire Barnabas Collins. We watched it every weekday after school on Channel 11. Wondered if Victoria would ever escape, if Barnabas would sink his teeth into her slender white neck. Would he ever set her free? Could he? It was clear he loved her. What Karen and I wanted to know, why we watched it every day, the question that was never answered: did she love him back?

Court Order

There was a court order. The only court I ever saw was on the *Perry Mason* show, where Perry and his assistant, a beautiful brunette woman, always convinced the jury that Perry was right. Perry was very clever and the brunette was very smart. And everyone always lived happily ever after on *Perry Mason*. But Perry Mason wasn't on the scene when the judge ordered my sisters and me to spend alternating weekends and most of the summer with my father and his new family. Even though we three broke no laws, never shoplifted, never murdered anyone, never lied on the stand, never even sat on the stand, we were sentenced, criminals by association.

Clean Dishes

For the last three years, it was my father I spent my time missing. Now it was my mother, alone in our home on Mayo Avenue. And even though it was only across town, it might as well have been a million miles away. Late at night, after my father and stepmother went to bed, my sisters and I called her. She never minded, talked all about Sam, how he sat by the back door waiting for us, how Sam and the cat had taken to sleeping together, which made us giggle. Then she said she was saving all the dirty dishes for us to wash when we got home. We laughed too, knowing how much our mother hated dirty dishes. That she would never let them collect in the sink. Never let us know that she wept each time she put her hands in the warm soapy water, the heat of it making her cry. One night she put the receiver up to Sam's face. We could hear his tongue slurping against our ears. Hear her laughing. "Just a few more weeks," she said. "Better hurry before I run out of clean dishes."

The House

He and Ann and the boys bought a house on an acre. We called it the summer house, not home. At first, my sisters and I tried to love her and her sons. We tried to love the house. We tried. Trying to love is harder than loving.

The Black Mare

What do you know? My father bought my sisters and me a horse to keep on the acre, a black mare who we adored even though she was swaybacked and stubborn. She was the bait, my father wanting so badly to make us happy. To give a reason for us to love his summers. I could at last be Dale Evans, Roy Rogers, Gene Autry, be a cowgirl true enough. She allowed my sisters and me, all three of us, to ride on her back at once, carried us through the woods and fields near his house. Took us away from Ann and her sons. We discovered that she would go faster if we sang, would pick up her head and cock her ears, her pace quickened. Her favorite was "Ninety-Nine Bottles of Beer on the Wall," a drinking song.

Makeup

In the morning, after the breakfast dishes were cleared away, Ann mixed her first, a gin and tonic. She had a red makeup case, with drawers that held small pots of color, soft pencils, tubes of creamy foundation that she squeezed onto her fingertips and smoothed across her cheeks. My sisters and I were hypnotized by her ritual, first the cotton ball with astringent, then the creams, the pressed powder, the lines drawn along her eyelids, the tiny comb she used to shape her dark eyebrows, the mascara, the odd instrument she used to make her eyelashes curl up. Then came the second and third. Sometimes after lunch, after the fourth, she'd remove the makeup and start over. She didn't drink alone. My father joined her.

Drinking

My mother never drank in the morning.

The Miles Between

Houston stretches and stretches. Our house near the Ship Channel, the one where my mother lived, our old home, was on the southern end, resting on low marshy ground, the soil black and thick, an hour's drive from the beach at Galveston where the muddy waves roll onto the brown sand, where your footprints vanish in the water's edge, where the salt air covers your skin like a thin chemise and shimmers there with Johnson's Baby Oil and loose sand. On the northern end, my father's house sat higher, near a patch of pine woods and a deep creek with a natural spring, the dirt red. He was north of the bayous, north of the oil refineries where both of my grandfathers worked, north of my friends and all that was familiar. It was only an hour away, but it could have been a lifetime, the black dirt just a memory.

Gardenias

Gardenias grow well in black dirt. My mother planted a bush beside our house, in a sunny spot that it loved, where it grew and grew, its leaves dark green and waxy, its soft petals white and fragrant. "This was the first thing I planted when we moved here," she told me one day. Turns out, she carried gardenias at her wedding.

The Gardener

She hired him to prune the trees and cut down the
gardenia bush.

Between Addresses

We all rode together: my father, Ann, the boys, us. We spent the hour in the car, squashed, three in front, four in back, all the spaces in between filled with cigarette smoke. The air filled with the end-of-summer. There was an ice house on Jones Road, halfway between addresses. They sold beer and boxes of Cracker Jack and my stepbrothers always asked for Dr Pepper. Halfway. There was condensation on the can of beer in my father's right hand. It looked like tears.

Long Division

He stood in the center. My father. Loved first by her. Then her boys who had him all the time now, more than us. On fall nights when my sisters and I weren't there, they came home from school and he helped them with their homework. When I was in the fourth grade, he showed me how to do long division, how to line up the numbers in columns going down the page, how to figure out the remainder. Sometimes the columns were so long, the numbers would start to fall off the page and then my father would show me how to make another column, straight, fine, one number folding into another, turning into a third number, an answer. Then there were the three of us, sisters. All loving him. But there was a remainder. My mother still loved him too.

What He Missed

The morning drive to school with the twins, Kevin and Keith, their mother taking us to Deady Junior High. How she told me every day that my skirt was too short, how I tugged on it. The way we laughed at Hudson and Harrigan, the crazy disc jockeys who gave the traffic report and told a story about someone called Little Elfie, a demented radio personality. How the Beatles sang "I Want to Hold Your Hand," while we traveled down Broadway to the redbrick building with its concrete gargoyles. The band concert, my silver flute gleaming under the lights. The party where Michael Harrison took my hand and kissed the top of it. The day home from school when Martin Luther King Jr. was shot and how my sisters and I watched television until dark while my mother worked. The way Sam got slower and slower. How I learned to make instant potatoes from a box. The field trip to the symphony where Karen and I sat next to each other and wrote notes while the trombone players stretched their slides to the end of the world and pulled them back again. The man my mother brought home to dinner twice a week. How he fried fish rolled in cornmeal for us and made all of us laugh. My mother's laugh. Sparkling. All of eighth grade. It's what he missed.

The Flutes

The silver flute was a gift from my mother. Each month she tore off a coupon, along with a check for ten dollars, and stuffed them into an envelope addressed to H&H Music Company. She couldn't afford it. So each night I played for her every song I knew. Then she bought one for Patti and B.J. too, prayed each month that the check to H&H wouldn't bounce. She never complained. Never told us how hard it was. Never walked out of the room when we played, silver notes drifting through the air. Silver linings.

The Clarinetist

My mother called it puppy love. Karen called it a
crush. But I knew it was more, this thing between the
clarinetist and me. It was bigger. It wrapped its arms
around me, soaked up all my energy, sat me down hard
and tugged at my bones and eyelids and every last inch
of every single cell. He was Michael Harrison. He
was beautiful. I couldn't get him out of my mind and
didn't want to anyway. He kissed me on the stairs after
school, and that was it, no more ground beneath my
feet, only air.

School Project

I had to turn in a project for Texas History, so decided to build a replica of the Old Stone Fort, a trading post in Nacogdoches, built in 1779 by a Frenchman. It's said that Davy Crockett spent the night there. I loved Davy Crockett, especially in the Disney version starring Fess Parker. Parker went on to portray Dan'l Boone too, but first he was Davy. Karen helped. We started with a cardboard box, coated it with paste made of flour, stuck dried red kidney beans in the paste. The beans were supposed to be the stones. They didn't look like stones. They looked like kidney beans. I took it to school and set it on a shelf near the window. After a couple of days the moisture from the paste made the beans sprout. If you listened carefully, you could hear them popping one at a time, the beans that is. My teacher gave me an A anyway, even though the other projects looked far better than mine and none of them sprouted. In a note to me she wrote, "True living history." This was just one project that my father never saw. Our histories were different.

The Clarinetist, Part 2

Karen was right about it being a crush. That's what it felt like when I saw him put his arms around a tall girl named Barbara. He didn't know I saw them. Or maybe he did. The crash landing was hard. *Crush* was the right word.

Films in P.E.

We had to get permission slips signed by our parents in order to see the films in P.E. Every seventh-grader lived for the end of the spring semester when we would finally get to see the films in P.E. Legend had it that each year someone fainted while watching the films in P.E. and often a teacher would have to assist a student who broke down while experiencing the films in P.E. Even teachers were known to swoon, so gripping were the films in P.E. Karen and I planned our wardrobe in advance, choosing our nicest clothes so that we would look mature for the viewing. We promised to sit next to each other in case one of us got woozy. Excitement was at a fever pitch as we filed into the auditorium. There were two films that day. The first was about dental hygiene and featured a beautiful teenage girl, all blond and cute. But nobody liked her because her breath was so bad. It was horrible, and she even contemplated suicide until her dentist intervened and taught her how to brush and floss and instructed her to get regular checkups. Her life was changed. She even got to be a cheerleader. The next film, a fifteen-minute animated description of menstruation, was riveting. It showed the lining of the uterine wall sloughing off and traveling down through the vagina, landing in a glob on a sanitary napkin. The big finale was actual photographs of Kotex pads (sans globs). Tampons were never mentioned. But there was a warning about how tacky it would be to have menstrual blood on the back of your skirt, so be prepared, always carry supplies with you, and pray that a prying boy doesn't rummage through your purse and find one and hold it up for all the world to see. How embarrassing would that be? On the way out, we were each given a new toothbrush.

Sand Castle

I could have been on my way to Galveston with Karen. Her family had invited me to spend the week there with them. At that very moment I would have been walking along the beach with her, looking for sharks' teeth and sand dollars on the edges of the waves, talking about how in love she was, thumbing through the pages of our new yearbook, building a sand castle with her little sister. At night her father would build a fire outside the cabin. We'd sit beside it and roast marshmallows, and he would sing "Waltzing Matilda" at the top of his voice. In the morning we'd help her mother bake gingerbread pancakes and wash the dishes. We'd take our towels and lie in the sun. We'd read and read and read, and then we'd talk about what we were reading. That's what we'd do. But summers belonged to him. Not me. Not Karen, or her boyfriend. So my sisters and I rode our black horse as far from his house as we could, until we got so thirsty we had to turn back, until we learned to take some sodas and cookies with us, carrots and apples for the horse, until we figured out how to bring summer to ourselves, how to give the horse her head.

Birthday, 1968

The first birthday without my mother.

Not the Only One

When you leave one parent for another, it's not only the absent parent you miss; it's your room, your pets, the clothes you leave in the closet. It was Karen. For a whole school year, we had spent every minute together, all our classes, our afternoons, our weekends. I missed her house too, the bedroom she shared with her sister, the table in her kitchen where we played Monopoly, her parents who laughed with us at dinner, her black piano where she played "Moonlight Sonata" by heart, the corner store where we pooled our money and shared a Fresca and a bag of barbecue potato chips after school. Karen was not a part of my father's household, and so a part of me wasn't either.

Birthday Continued, 1968 – Fourteen

Ivory-colored boots, Tony Lama, made of kangaroo
hide and as soft as velvet; they hugged my feet like a
second skin. When I opened the box they were in on my
birthday, Ann started telling me how to take care of
them, how to use the special leather cream that was
tucked inside the box, how it would keep them soft so
that the leather wouldn't dry and crack, like a woman's
hands tend to do when they've done so many loads of
laundry, like the dirt does when it needs rain, like a wall
when the house has shifted. It was nice of her to tell me.
My heart sang at the sight of them, knowing how
expensive they were, knowing that my father had special-
ordered them. How they made me feel like the queen of
the rodeo. The way it was when I found a pair just like
them in his closet one day while helping my stepmother
put away the dry cleaning. Only they were hers. Just like
mine. Not mine. She took all of him, didn't she? The
next time our church held a rummage sale to raise money

for a new stove, I donated the boots worn maybe three times, not even broken in, along with the special cream to keep them soft tucked inside the left one. The pastor told me they brought a nice sum. But not enough to buy back a birthday, not enough to special-order a father, not enough to keep the skin from cracking.

Not the First

They weren't the first pair of cowboy boots I ever had,
no. My first pair were red with white stitching. They
matched my red leather skirt and vest, the ones with the
fringe. It all came in a box with cellophane on the top
that you could see through. I was four or five. I was Dale
Evans. I could make black scuff marks on the kitchen
floor. I could gallop faster than the wind. I could round
up strays. Settle the West. Those were my first.

Rings

My stepmother couldn't help but wipe the kitchen counter over and over. When she sat on the stool next to the bar, she held her drink, a gin and tonic, in one hand. In the other she held a sponge. Each time she raised her glass to her mouth, she wiped the wet ring left behind on the counter where it so recently sat. She did the same for our Coca-Colas, my stepbrothers' orange juice. She was at war with the rings on the counter, with the dust on the furniture, with the dirt under my stepbrothers' fingernails. My sisters and I stayed out of the kitchen until he got home from work. We must have made her nervous, we three with our court order and our sweaty bottles of soda. Here it was summer again, and the invisible judge had brought us together. What a happy family! If the judge were to visit, I'd serve him up a gin and tonic and see if she would take her sponge after his rings each time he took a sip.

Before, Once Again

The pony's name was Soot because he looked as if he had been coated in ashes. I loved him immediately even though he wasn't mine, but the man's who ran the stable on Telephone Road, not really a stable but a lean-to with three concentric rings. For twenty-five cents you could ride a pony around one of the rings three times, three spins for a quarter. On Saturdays he took us there, my sisters and me. From Sunday through Friday, I waited, dreamed pony dreams. He wasn't mine, but I loved him nonetheless. And so I was sorry when the man moved, took his ponies, loaded them in a large van, and moved to the country, a better place for ponies than Telephone Road. The rings were left behind, as empty as the rings around the moon, as circular as my father's wedding ring, the one he lost in Arabia so many years later.

Summer Uncle

My stepmother's brother was a full-time mechanic and part-time bull rider, an "uncle," I guess. On summer weekends, he rode at the Aldine Rodeo, just off the interstate not far from his house. I loved the rodeo smell: livestock, leather, popcorn, fresh dirt. I watched the high-school girls ride in on their beautiful horses, each holding a flag, one for America, one for Texas, watched them gallop around the arena, their horses' tails flying, their lamé outfits glittering in the lights. I wanted to be a rodeo queen too. But our black mare, her swayback, wasn't cut out for lights and arenas. Usually Ann's brother made a little money, said the bulls were chosen just for him. Not always, not every time. He was a nice man too. Whenever he made some cash, he bought everyone a hamburger afterward at the Whataburger. In the end, he earned a big belt buckle made of silver and bronze, champion of the Aldine Rodeo, nieces in the stands. A hero. My father loved him too, loved to talk about cars with him, loved to walk into his garage and help him pull out an engine or change someone's oil, loved to throw back a beer with him and recite the poems of Robert Service. The two of them seemed to rhyme: her brother, my father. He was only one of all these relatives who weren't but were, my father the connecting link. The summer uncle—mechanic, bull rider, poet.

True Uncle

I had a true uncle too, who made gumbo, starting with a roux of flour and bacon grease, and adding in the salt pork and okra and peeled shrimp and crab and tomatoes and all the secret ingredients he never divulged and then boiled it up in a huge pot that bubbled and brewed and hissed until it was rich and thick and brown as the bayous and he spooned it over bowls of steamy white rice, as white as sun-bleached sheets, and oh, how my mouth sang. He was my mother's brother. It was a recipe handed down from a tugboat captain he met in the Marines, who disappeared in the Louisiana swamp one day and never came back. This is what my true uncle said. Said the gumbo would make you fall in love, it was that spicy.

The Slide Show

One night, before we went home to our mother and the approaching school year, he hung an old sheet on the living-room wall with thumbtacks, pulling the corners tight so that it didn't sag. Then he invited all his neighbors for a slide show. My youngest stepbrother sat in his lap and got to push the forward button. My other stepbrother turned off the light. They called him Bill. We called their father Mr. Scarmardo. Suddenly the wall was splashed with color. Then he was the most exotic father in Texas. The proof was in the slides: camels, men in white gowns, women in black, faces covered by long-fingered hands, olive trees, date palms, pistachios. The best: my father atop a camel, the desert sun beaming from his green aviator glasses, the Persian Gulf gleaming in the distance—he was my one and only Lawrence of Arabia. And there were slides and slides of people kneeling on woven mats. *Allah,* they called through the silent film. It seemed my father couldn't believe it, men in white, women in black, bent in half on the sandy ground facing Mecca in uneven rows. Even now, when I think of Arabia, it's camels and praying that come to me, my father's fascination, all those prayers on his living-room wall.

Her Hair

Her hair fell to her shoulders in waves, black, thick; unlike mine, straight, blond, thin. She combed it back, away from her face, which was sharp, her mouth drawn down. She rarely smiled. I walked into the kitchen one day and caught her weeping, her head back, the tears streaming into her hair. When she saw me, she started laughing, like it was something funny she was crying about. "What is it?" I asked. "Something got me," she said. My father had a *National Geographic* magazine on the coffee table, and when I turned to a photograph of an old ship, the carved face on the prow looked like hers, the thick hair, the salty tears, the head held back, the ancient yearning to sail away. It got me.

More of Before

Peppermint Park. It sat right next to the new Gulf Freeway, not too far from Mayo Avenue. There was a small roller coaster and a carousel and a house of mirrors and bumper cars and pinball games and shuffleboard. My parents took us there with my cousins. I pretended it was enchanted and the horse I rode on the carousel, a huge black stallion with carved ribbons in his mane and tail, his head thrown back, was racing, racing, flying past the chain-link fence, the parked cars, the shopping center across the road. We went so fast that when we passed my parents, their faces were a blur, all their edges soft. I let go and rode without any hands, knowing that my steed would never toss me, never harm me, never throw me to the ground. When the carousel stopped, there were fireflies in the air. My father lifted me to the ground. "How was it, Old Bean?" he asked. I patted the wooden horse, rubbed my hand across his ear. "Wonderful," I whispered.

Steps

I had titles: stepdaughter, stepsister. I had additional
relatives: stepmother, stepbrothers, even stepgrand-
parents and stepaunts and -uncles and stepcousins.
There were steps here and steps there. My sisters and
I stepped from one house to another. We were stairsteps.
We were steps one through three. We stepped lightly.
Two steps forward, one step back. We stepped high and
low. One missed step led to them all. A step in the right
direction became a step off the cliff. Step by step by
step. "Step away, mister," said John Wayne to the bad
guy. "Take a step," says the mother to the baby. "Step
outside," says the county sheriff to the driver. Step up or
lose your bearings. Step on a crack, break your mother's
back. Watch your step—the main idea.

High School

Ninth grade: football games, marching in the band, "Hey Jude" on the radio, Richard Nixon in the White House, and the city-bus ride to downtown Houston with Karen to shop at Foley's on a Saturday and have lunch at the counter at Walgreen's. Ninth grade: a game of spin the bottle, and a kiss that sent me clean through the solar system, a kiss with a boy named Joe who played drums in the band. It was Advanced Algebra and *A Tale of Two Cities* and a report for World Geography about Lipizzan horses, typed on my grandmother's old Royal typewriter. It was my mother's new job, a better one, better pay, better hours. Better. Ninth grade. Franco Zeffirelli made *Romeo and Juliet*, a promise that love could be true. I wanted to buy that in the ninth grade.

Speaking Of . . .

. . . there was that brief frame, early in the morning, the soft light slipping through the window, settling upon Leonard Whiting's beautiful naked body, Juliet beside him, peaceful, serene, the music as lush as the lighting, as if Zeus himself had arranged the whole thing and not Franco Zeffirelli, and it didn't matter one way or the other because Leonard Whiting's beautiful naked body carved itself on my brain, a temple of a body, as if his beautiful naked body was the holiest thing in the world.

Once More, Before

In Hempstead, a tiny dot on the map, just west of Houston, the farmers grow watermelons so large they look like boats. They're called black diamonds. Each year there's a Watermelon Festival on the second Saturday in July. We went there when I was small, listened to a gospel choir sing tunes about Jesus, and ate watermelon so cold it made my cheeks numb. There was a seed-spitting contest and a little boy with dark eyes, younger than I, maybe five, spit a seed almost twenty feet, spit it in a perfect straight line, hard to believe. My father bought a black diamond that day, brought it home with us, tucked it on the floorboards in front of us, so large that all six of our bare feet rested on its cool green rind. Once home, he set it on the front porch. The next day it was gone, heisted. It was a mystery to my father why anyone would steal a watermelon. "I can't believe it," he kept saying. That morning in church, I prayed to Jesus to find the watermelon, but what's a watermelon to the son of God? What's a black diamond to a believer?

Ann Landers Tells the Difference

I wanted to know, but didn't know who to ask, so imagine my surprise when Ann Landers used her column to explain who was a virgin and who wasn't. Down to the details. My mother used to say, "God is in the details." Ann Landers gave God a whole new spin.

Birthday, 1969 – Fifteen

Another birthday without my mother. She called early, before she went to work, sang "Happy Birthday" over the phone, made Sam lick the receiver, promised we would have another party when I came home, said my grandmother was taking a course in cake decorating, so it was good that we had to wait to celebrate since the course wasn't finished yet. They still had to learn roses. I wanted roses. Pink roses. Red roses. Yellow roses. Spun sugar atop a cake so white it made you blink. "Yes," I said, "I want roses."

Birthday, 1969, Again

What I really wanted was to see Karen, to walk across the street to her house, to watch her play "Moonlight Sonata" on her piano and hear her tell me about how Beethoven was deaf when he wrote it. I wanted to sit at her kitchen table and work the crossword puzzle together. I wanted to watch *Gidget Goes Hawaiian* on her television, with her sister and brother too. I wanted to get back into my regular skin, the one I wore when I was at home, where I wasn't a stepdaughter or a stepsister, where I was just Karen's friend, myself.

Birthday, 1969, Finally

It was a complete set of Merle Norman skin-care products, including a special foundation that was tinted green and a bottle of astringent that stung my cheeks when I applied it with a cotton ball. It was my step-mother's idea. "The green tint gives balance to your natural skin color," she said. I couldn't wait. All the bottles and tubes and brushes lined neatly inside a pink carrying case with a mirror that popped up when it was opened. I took it into the bathroom where I applied each product according to the directions, carefully cleaned my face with the special soap, then tenderly rubbed in the green-tinted foundation, smoothing it over my chin, my forehead, beneath my eyes. I did look balanced. There was eye shadow, eye liner, mascara, a whole bounty of beauty products. The face in the mirror didn't even look like me. I looked radiant. I could be on the cover of *Seventeen* magazine even though I was only fifteen. It was wonderful for the hour before the skin on my face began to itch. Everyone said I looked lovely, like a cover girl, like a model. I wondered if cover girls' faces itched under the hot lights. Then if they could stand it, so could I, but I only lasted another hour when I couldn't get it all off quickly enough. The face in the mirror was bright red, the eyes puffy, the tissue in my hand soft green, balanced.

Before, Once at Halloween

My mother took three of my father's old shirts and cut them up so that they looked worn and tattered, took them out to the yard and stomped on them, an added touch of grime. At the local 7-Eleven store she bought us each a bamboo cane and tied bandannas around the ends, stuffed them with apples and old rags. It was Halloween and my sisters and I were hoboes for the night. She smudged our faces with her charcoal eye shadow and let us wear her old shoes which flopped on our feet as we walked. It was hard for us to look pathetic, so happy were we to be authentic beggars, so glad to have real costumes and not the store-bought kind that looked like everybody else's store-bought kind. My father came home from work, expressed mock dismay at the loss of his shirts, found his flashlight, and followed us from house to house, shining the light ahead so that we wouldn't trip in our clunky shoes. When we got back to our house, my mother greeted us at the door, handed us each a cup of hot cocoa and my father a beer. In return, he kissed her and reached for her hand. "Trick or treat," he said, and kissed her again.

On Halloween Before That Halloween

Before the hobo Halloween, there was one when we were so small my father carried B.J. from house to house. I wore a Sylvester (the cat) costume, and Patti was Tweety Bird. B.J. just wore her baby clothes. Patti didn't say, "Trick or treat." She just said, "Tweet." They would open the door, and at the top of her lungs, "Tweeet!" Pretty soon, my father started saying it too. And then me. The door would open. "Tweet!" Everyone laughed. For years after that, every Halloween, my father said that one was his favorite, how all the neighbors laughed, how he held B.J. in his arms, how there weren't any ghosts that night or even stars, just a father and his three daughters shouting "Tweeet" as loud as we could.

Home

Home is more than a place. When you are forced to leave one for another, home is a yearning, always just beneath the surface, inside your pores, along the edges of the long humid days. He even built a garage apartment for us so that we had our own special place, let us hang a black light, shine it on neon posters, let us choose the bedspreads and the carpet, the tile for the bathroom, let us keep our stepbrothers out, gave us each a key. We could stay up all night, sleep as late as we wanted, play the music so loud the window shook. And we did. Steppenwolf through the night. Home the other side of town.

Someone New

An interesting thing happened between summers. My mother found someone too, not the man who fried fish— he was short—rather, a tall man with dark hair and glasses, not at all like my father, suddenly my stepfather, so when we left for his house, she wasn't so sad to see us go.

Happiness Flipped

It was funny, in a way. Here was my mother, so happy, after being so blue. Here was my father, happiness slipping away, drowning in gin and beer. I noticed that he left the room whenever Ann walked in. I saw that she followed him, her voice tinged with anger. She bought a baby raccoon and raised it on a bottle, carried it with her everywhere, took it in the car with her. At first so small it fit in a coffee cup. No one was allowed to touch it, even though its fur was softer than air.

Before All This

"It doesn't hurt! It doesn't hurt!" the boy next door to my grandmother shouted in his desperate voice. He shouted it to my baby sister, B.J., whose screams brought my grandmother running to her side. She was holding her small round stomach with her small round hands. Her face was a storm: tears, snot, saliva rained onto the ground. "Let me see, let me see," coaxed my grandmother, prying B.J.'s hands from her stomach. There, lodged next to her bellybutton, embedded in the flesh, a small, round BB. "It doesn't hurt!" the boy shouted. Then he cried too. My grandmother sent him home, took B.J. inside, pried the BB out with tweezers, and set it in her hand: a prize. She was three. My other sister, Patti, was four. I was five. Some things just hurt.

Sisters

It was a good time to have sisters, to have each other, to speak in regular voices, play our flutes. We could have brought friends with us to his house. "They are always welcome," he said. And sometimes they came; sometimes they rode with us across the bayous, past the tall buildings, down Interstate 45 until it became just two lanes and we exited onto Hwy 1960, a small general store on the right, the only grocery store for miles. Houston claimed it was in the city limits, but it didn't feel that way. No traffic lights or skyscrapers. The black mare swished her tail and hung her head over the fence when we pulled into the drive. One year at Easter someone gave my father a peacock to keep in his backyard. It didn't stay there, preferring the pine woods next to his house. At night it screamed, its high-pitched cry piercing the air. "It sounds like a woman being beaten," said Ann. I had never heard a woman being beaten, but I believed her. "Your friends are always welcome," said my father. Sometimes they came. But it was mostly us—three sisters.

Enchantment

We were enchanted with the raccoon, its tiny hands as dexterous as ours. Its eyes as shiny as glass. He was like an elf, a tiny mischief-maker, pulling tricks on the household. He unplugged the lamps, unrolled the toilet paper, hid the keys, climbed the drapes, teased the dog. When Ann sat down in the living-room chair, he climbed into her lap and snuggled into her arms. She allowed him to sit on the kitchen counters, to curl up in the cabinets with the dishes, to rummage through the pantry, chewing through boxes of oatmeal and Kellogg's Frosted Flakes. "He shouldn't have been teasing it," she said, when it bit Danny on the foot, a deep slash that required twelve stitches. As the raccoon grew, it got meaner and meaner. No one could go near it except Ann, and then one day it bit her too, bit her hard on the hand. My father had it put down, and she didn't get out of bed for days. We could hear her crying through the closed door of their bedroom. "It's the flu," my father said. He carried her another gin and tonic, poured one for himself. We stayed in our garage apartment, spun records, felt sorry for the raccoon.

Before Before

When I was in the second grade, he took me to visit
the library at Rice University. Just he and I one
Saturday. It was a long walk from our car to the huge
building. I wore my best velvet dress. The day was crisp,
bright, a fall day. We walked between a row of marble
columns and through the large wooden doors. I had
never seen so many books. He held my hand and we
walked between every row until I got dizzy from the rush
of books going by. Until I had to sit down. He didn't
have a library card, wasn't a student at Rice. "I think you
might go here someday," he told me. I didn't know then
how much he was saying to me. Didn't know how much
he wanted all those books to be mine, to have a library
card. He didn't go to college, you see. Instead, he
became a father.

Sweet Sixteen, 1970

"Never been kissed" wasn't true. Sixteen brought with it a boy, a sweet boy with brown hair and deep brown eyes, a boy who played the trumpet, who was thinner than a rail, who loved to work on old cars and spent Saturdays working at the Texaco station next to our high school, and who took me to see Three Dog Night in concert and called me almost every night, who told funny jokes and ran his fingers along the edge of my chin. Who kissed me.

Birthday Continued, 1970

He took us downtown to eat—Karen, me, the boy—
then to Market Square where all the hippies sold their
black-light posters and patchouli incense, where they
wore their hair in long braids down their backs and sat in
circles on the square. Good-bye, Rodeo Girl. I wanted to
be one of them, a flower child, wear white eyeliner with
blue mascara on my eyes, made by Love, imported from
England, land of Joe Cocker and the Beatles and Mick
Jagger, where no one could get any satisfaction. I knew
every song by the Bee Gees, could sing every line, loved
them all, wanted to dance forever at 45 revolutions per
minute, knew their names, knew that flowers looked
lovely in my hair.

Before, Once More

My mother gave him a ukulele because he loved the
Kingston Trio, so on summer evenings he sat in his lawn
chair on the front stoop of our house on Mayo Avenue
and sang, "Hang down your head, Tom Dooley / Hang
down your head and cry," over and over. My sisters and I
sang along. One evening the man across the street
brought out a pair of bongo drums and his lawn chair
and his two kids, our best friends. There was a washtub
full of beer, Black Label, with a church key tied to the
handle on a string. As the stars slowly popped out, they
sang other songs too: "Day-O" and "Bottle of Wine"
and "The Streets of Laredo." But every three or four
songs they'd go back to "Tom Dooley," hang down their
heads, and cry.

The War

On the other side of the world, there was a war.
Fought in jungles and rice paddies. We saw it on the
television every night, saw soldiers slogging through the
mud, carrying their broken buddies on their shoulders.
There was a war at the house on the acre, more quiet, as
desperate. The summer slowed into a sorry march
through its own long days, the Houston sun scorching
every blade of grass, every azalea bush. It was too hot to
saddle the black mare who stood beneath a shady group
of winged elm trees, so still she might have been a statue.
To step outside was to hear the gasping hum of air
conditioners straining to keep pace with the heat,
slogging through the humid hours, until finally, toward
evening, the sun conceded control to the night, barely.
Barely cooler, but enough to wander into the backyard
and breathe in air that wasn't refrigerated. My father
took residence atop the redwood picnic table, cool beer
in his hand, tired from working all day, tired from the

dinner conversation with its bits of code that circled over our heads, spat into the air, word missiles. Ann stayed in the house, simmering. Stepbrothers rode their bikes up and down the gravel drive, on leave. My sisters and I, in between, longed for this summer to end, hated to leave our father again, so sad. But then there was the boy. And there were the kisses. And they were on the other side of town, waiting.

Promises

Karen loved Mike, who was taller than she was. He gave her a promise ring. A promise to be true. A promise to be steady. A promise to shower her with kisses. I was jealous for a while, no promise ring for me. But Mike broke his promise and kissed someone else. So the two of us sat up all night and played backgammon and ate popcorn until dawn, when we climbed onto her roof and watched the sun rise. Two girls in our nightgowns, dew settling on our skin. The sun is cold so early in the morning.

There It Was

I loved the boy with the brown hair.

Drowning

I've been told there are several ways to drown. "You can drown," my mother warned, "in a half inch of water." Another is in a sea of sorrow. Bathtubs, it turns out, are popular places to drown. A can of beer was my father's choice. My stepmother preferred gin.

The War Continued

Before I came along, my father jumped out of airplanes. He was a member of the Eighty-second Airborne, a parachute jumper. The Korean War ended just after he enlisted, so he never saw any action. Never had to stand knee-deep in a muddy foxhole. Never had to watch his buddies disintegrate beside him. Never came under enemy fire. At the house on the acre, there was no place to jump.

Gunslingers

My sisters and I knew all the famous TV gunslingers:
Wyatt Earp, Doc Holliday, Bat Masterson, John Wayne,
and of course Chuck Conners, the Rifleman. Knew how
they kept the West in line. They could pull those guns,
fire those triggers, fell the evil outlaws before the rest of
us could blink. Funny thing, though, we never saw Miss
Kitty draw a gun, never saw her lily-white hands touch
the cold metal of a revolver or a Colt .45. So it was a
surprise when Ann shot my father in the backyard of
their one-acre house.

Once Before

Other people have been shot. When I was in the fourth grade, my mother sent my sisters and me to school with rollers in our hair. At noon, she picked us all up and took us home where we put on our nicest dresses. It was November, late, the air was crisp, just a few days before Thanksgiving. My father came home too. All this in the middle of the day, a school day. We drove across town and parked the car, then got out and joined thousands of other people, all of us lining the street, Broadway, all of us in our best clothes, my father in his suit and tie, my mother with her high heels. "Hold hands," my mother yelled, as the crowd pushed us forward. My father lifted my youngest sister onto his shoulders and Patti and I held hands as tightly as we could. Somehow, the two of us pushed forward to the street itself. We were right on the curb, our parents behind us. The street was empty, not a single car. It wasn't like the rodeo parade where there were clowns

170

and cowboys, a flatbed trailer draped with crepe paper and pulled by a John Deere. We waited and waited, the street eerily quiet. At last a roar started to rise from the crowd—or was it from the motorcycle police who were coming toward us, coming from the direction of the airport? They drove slowly so we could see them clearly, see their stern faces, their leather straps beneath their chins. Then came a black convertible with a man and a woman sitting up on the back. "It's the mayor," said my mother. He was followed by another and another, until at last, the final car. My mother started crying. "Wave!" she shouted. We did, our hands clothed in small white cotton gloves, one finger wet from chewing on it. And he waved back, the rider in the last car, John F. Kennedy, Jackie on the seat beside him. They waved directly at us, right at me and Patti, at my sister B.J. atop my father's shoulders, at my mother crying, my father smiling. I could see his face clearly, eyes, ears, nose, chin, facing my way, his wide mouth in a grin, so familiar, the face of a thousand photographs. The next morning, in the paper, the president was quoted as saying how happy he was to have had such a warm welcome from the folks in Houston. The next day he went to Dallas.

A Big Mistake

I guess the reason Miss Kitty never got to shoot the gun is that she had such a bad aim. When the gunslingers hit their targets, they always died. My father didn't die. And my stepmother didn't go to jail. He told the police that he had returned home unexpectedly, without warning, and she had mistaken him for an intruder. "Just a big mistake," he said. He put his hand over his eyes and sobbed.

Mistake, Reprise

It wasn't like an addition error on your algebra test. It wasn't like forgetting to dot an *i* or cross a *t*. It wasn't like leaving the salt out of the spaghetti sauce.

Years Before

My grandmother had a chair that spun in circles. It was short and round and covered in nubby brown upholstery. We took turns. One sister sat on the round, overstuffed seat while the other two of us gripped the bottom edge and spun the chair around and around, faster and faster until the riding sister was just a blur. Then she stepped off, wobbled, crossed one foot over the other, balance thrown completely off. We pretended we were drunk, slurred our speech, collapsed in a heap on the living-room carpet, for a moment the world a spinning top, bouncing into the furniture, tilting off the walls, every blink of the eye a swirl of color. It was like that at my father's house, each toss of the bottle another loss of equilibrium.

The Boy with the Brown Hair

When a girl falls in love, sometimes the falling is hard, and sometimes it's soft. My own falling was soft, cushioned by a million kisses. Kisses between classes. Kisses at the football game. Kisses in the backseat of an old Ford. On the bus to the beach. At the drive-in movie. In the middle of a rainstorm. Sweet, sweet kisses. A million. Maybe more.

Driving Lessons

On Sundays, when the shopping mall was closed, my father taught me how to drive in the parking lot. It was a Cougar, the car, emerald green, my stepmother's favorite color. Around and around we drove, up and down between the concrete markers, fast, slow, stop, start, forward, reverse. It was freedom, the car, the road in front of me, my father stepping out and letting me go.

Gone Again

"I'm leaving," he said, his voice cracking over the phone. He didn't know how long he'd be gone. Couldn't say when he'd be back. So my father's summers ended when he went back to Arabia, back to the shifting sands and burly camels. He stayed two more years, and would not come home until I graduated, Class of 1972. No more required summers at his house, no more watching my stepmother wipe off the kitchen counters every five minutes, no more. I missed him a little, missed the way he called me "Old Bean," missed the black mare.

My Stepfather

I might have missed him more. But there was George. There was the sweet way he danced with my mother in the living room, then twirled each of my sisters and me around too. There was the way he held his head back and "woofed" with his two dogs, Clyde and Booker, until all of us were howling. There was his old Lincoln Continental that sat in the driveway and never budged, just sat there, rusty and forlorn, but loved nonetheless. There was his ability to build a cabinet or fix a pipe, to varnish a table or stop a leak, to read a poem out loud so that each word was round and perfect and wonderful. There was George. Generous. Strong. In love with my mother. His love so big that we fit there too.

Sometime Before

I think it was the third grade, fall, the music teacher
formed a choir. It was her job to direct the Autumn
Program at Pearl Rucker Elementary School. The theme
was the "Old West." I was thrilled. She chose five of us
to sit on the stage around a pretend campfire and strum
ukuleles. Because I had my father's ukulele, I got to be
one of the five. We wore jeans and cowboy shirts, with
vests that had fringe on them, and red cowboy hats. On
the night of the program, the construction-paper
campfire blazed. I knew all my chords, had practiced
them over and over, just the way the music teacher had
shown me. I could play them without looking down,
place my fingers just right on the frets so that the strings
wouldn't buzz. All the seats were taken. My mother and
sisters, my grandmother and grandfather, my uncle,
everyone was there. Except my father. The program
started. I played. The choir sang. I looked across the
room, filled to the brim with smiling faces, none of them

his. I focused on the campfire, stayed in its orange paper flames. As we finished the final song, I looked up and saw him, slipping through the double doors at the back of the cafeteria, just in front of the ice-cream cooler. All the verses were finished. All the chords played. Afterward he told me, "It was wonderful, Bean." And mostly, it was.

Birthday, 1971 — Seventeen

The boy with the brown hair gave me a bouquet of soft pink gladioli, their petals so thin, I could almost see through them. From the Persian Gulf, I got a check for twenty dollars. "Wish I knew what to get you, Bean," he wrote. I spent it on a pair of blue jeans that I wore low on my hips, a pair that had wide bell bottoms that frayed at the bottom with each step I took; that, should I step out of them, I might burst into flames.

Calls

"I talked to your father," she said. Ann's voice, sharp and clear, popped through the telephone receiver. Every so often, she called, usually late, the phone's ring piercing the night. I could always tell it was her. Her ring had a particular edge to it. The conversation was always the same, how he was not coming home yet, how he missed us, asked about his girls, how she didn't care, how she knew he loved us more than her, how it didn't matter, she was fine, better than ever, now that he was gone, how she had given up everything for him, how her boys wanted him to come back, how she felt like killing herself: "Don't hang up, or I'll do it," she said. How my stepfather gently took the phone from my hand and quietly told her didn't she think it was a little late to be calling. She never answered him, just hung up.

Graduation

When my father graduated from high school, he was given a book—*Rudyard Kipling: Complete Verse: Definitive Edition.* There's a poem, "Mandalay," that he read to me from the time I was four, a poem about flying fishes and the sun coming up like thunder, and China, and a woman the poet so loved that he would do anything to see her again. There's a road in the poem. There are roads in our hearts, those that take us away, those that bring us home, those that lead to anywhere and nowhere. My father traveled on all of them, and one of those was back to me on my graduation night. He held the book, and then gave it to me with a note. "Dad" was all it said. Its red cover was marred by the many drinks he set on it, the melting ice cubes on the insides of the glasses making wet rings on the outsides, engraving themselves into the cloth, a history of gin and tonics. When I pressed the

book against my face, I could smell his fingers, the
Camel cigarettes he smoked. When I read the poems out
loud, I heard the poet's heartbeat in the rhythms and
rhymes, the British Empire ringing in my ears. When I
turned the thin pages, I could feel the fishes flying by.

Birthday, 1972–Eighteen

Eighteen brings a vote, doesn't it? At campaign head-quarters I was given a button with a white dove on it, the sign of peace. Come fall, I would vote for McGovern. In the meantime, I voted for the boy and all those kisses. Voted for long walks at the beach. Moved into my own body, apart from my mother and father and sisters and all those summer relatives. Voted to let go. Voted to hold on. Voted to fly.

Karen, for Sure

There was no letting go of Karen, but our paths went different ways. She stayed in Houston and I didn't. But we knew how to be friends with miles between. We had practiced. We were good at it.

Dorm Room

I barely remember the trip from Houston to College Station, the one hundred miles, my pink Samsonite suitcase so full I could barely close it, the suitcase a graduation gift. He and my stepmother smoked all the way there so that when I stepped out of the car in front of my dorm, it billowed out, a cloud coming to rest by the street's curb. My room was on the fourth floor, no elevators, and he carried that pink suitcase up every stair, then went back for the five cardboard boxes that held my bed linens and books and stuffed animals. He wanted to take me to lunch then, wanted just a few more minutes before he left, wanted to take a tour of the campus where he was dropping me, me, me and all my five boxes, here to stay, at least for a while. He didn't press when I said no. No lunch. No moments. No tour. So long, Dad. So long.

Divorce Again

By the end of my freshman year, they were divorced, my father and Ann. She moved out of the house on the acre and took her two boys with her. My father went back to Arabia, a place more home than home, and continued to send me letters on thin paper, letters that started, "Dear Bean . . . ," and always ended with "Love always."

Something Else

Something else continued: the phone calls. At first, just calling to say hello, how she always thought of me as her daughter, no, as her friend, and wasn't my father coming home soon, and there were things I didn't know that if I only knew and it might have been different if it weren't for "you girls," you always came first, and how much he talked about us until she thought she might go crazy and weren't her sons driving her crazy and wasn't it all so crazy, and who did my mother think she was and how are your classes and wouldn't it be funny if I just killed myself, maybe everyone would be happier . . . "Don't hang up or I'll kill myself. . . ."

Much Later, Years

Long, long after, many years later, she did it. She killed herself. Nobody was happier.

Connection

When a daughter lives in Texas and a father lives in Arabia, she learns to look at the moon and believes that he has looked at it and thought of her. It may seem silly, but the moon doesn't laugh at her or even smile. It simply shines.

Way Before

I have a photograph of my father, his blond hair combed to the side. He's standing in the sun without a shirt, holding me, a toddler, in his arms. He's very thin and his pants are very baggy. He looks like a boy, too young to be a father, and he was too, only nineteen. He's looking at me looking out, looking toward the camera. His face is shining, his smile is sweet. It's clear he's happy to be holding me, hanging on to me. Despite everything, that was always clear.

Family Photos

(The Rainbow Girls are a junior service organization sponsored by the Masons. My grandfather was a Mason for more than sixty years; I was a Rainbow Girl in seventh and eighth grades.)